T0146616

My Iron Butterfly

JAEVEL BROWN

MY IRON BUTTERFLY

iUniverse books may be ordered through booksellers or by contacting:

iUniverse
1663 Liberty Drive
Bloomington, IN 47403
www.iuniverse.com
1-800-Authors (1-800-288-4677)

ISBN: 978-1-5320-6562-0 (sc)
ISBN: 978-1-5320-6563-7 (e)

Print information available on the last page.

iUniverse rev. date: 12/27/2018

To my family,
My complete joy

And to every person who ever inspired me to write

Contents

Family Matters

The World and I

God & I

Sadness & Grief

Acknowledgments

To all the beautiful souls in my life that I do not have space enough to name, whose love for and faith in me, brought me to the printing of this completed work.

To God, for still giving me days and breaths to try and make the next one more meaningful.

Thank you!

A poem is less interested in
meeting the expectations of others
than it is in saying what it was meant to say.
A poet writes simply because they must.
Poetry is therefore the product
of intrepid necessity.

- Jaevel Brown

Family Matters

Iron Butterfly

She is heavy from the war
Weighted, mechanical
She has lost the poetry in her wings
Her soul wears armor now
The sun no longer cools and inspire
It only makes hot
The rain has lost its sweet caress
It now rusts and cuts
Colors danced on her skin
Beauty once adorned her freedom -
Now, she hides from the wind
She sits by her shadow
Weighted, mechanical
She has lost the poetry in her wings
Will you see the rainbow as it was?
Have you now forgotten the glory of the past?
The hope of future?
No, you must not forget!
Get up and fly!
Broken and tired you may be
Weighted, mechanical perhaps
But you have need to meet the sky
For I look for you there
My iron butterfly

Aunty Kisses

Why do you kiss me aunty
When I want to tell you about the world?
Tell you of all the beauty I see?
There are rainbows swinging from the tree tops and birds singing in
harmony with the voice of the forest
Sand and rain and breeze and streams hug this restless, weary earth.
But, how very beautiful the glory I see
In awe of Him who composed my birth

Why do you stop me dear aunty, why do you cradle my fall?
When I know the best of lessons to be learnt are gained when I risk it all?
Do not teach me fear aunty
Though I know it is not your intention
Don't let me learn to stay behind invisible lines
And stifle my potential
I hear your love aunty
I see it in your eyes
But learn to love me with open arms
And make your worries subside

The world is only big for now aunty
And there are places I'll have to go
But near or far, I will remember still
The aunty that loves me so

For Them

Them, I can't love with a heart
They will never be my heartbeat
I can't love them with a whisper or a shout
For them, love can claim no comparison to the depths of the ocean
Nor promise of continuity after death
It will never be as the wind, flowers or sky
This love for them will always say goodbye
And that's ok.
For it is after a goodbye that the best hellos come
This love loves here and now;
At every time, for every time – always
However deep the seas go, there is still an ocean floor
This love has no bottom, nor looks down
It looks up at the vastness of the world undiscovered beyond the blue
This love is not a hush nor a bellow
But the sweet quietude of a poet fellow
They will never be my heartbeat
It races, slows down and is unsteady
It will cease one day in fright or rest
But the love for this Them I proclaim
Will never

Sonnet I

Two sides of a coin
Two choruses to a song
Every measure of a man
Every need to belong
Someone colored by today
And prepares for battle tomorrow
A soul who is hungry for joy
Who buries his own sorrow
There's a hug hung on the windowsill
Gazing out into the sunset
Waiting for his figure to appear
Anxious with warmth he won't forget
But, he doesn't break the horizon –
Maybe sometime soon
He'll come before December's end
Humming his favorite tune

Sonnet II

I can't imagine the sound of your heart breaking
Nor vision tears running down your face
Must be like the sound of a fetus praying
Hoping for the world to be a better place
Perhaps you cry in heaven first
And the clouds dry your eyes
Each drop worth more than a rich lass' purse
Emotions reserved to be an angel's prize
I've glimpsed your smile though
In the picture across the street
Past the corner of indifference
Where a brother and sister meet
I've framed that sketch with my heart
It will be on show all my days
The captured view of my brother laughing
And the boy at play it betrays

You Should Know

You will never know how much I love you
And how much I wish that was enough
How exceptional I know you are
How brilliant and brave
You inspire me every day
In so many ways
Will this world ever know?
Will they ever see your great?
How sad it must be for them
How much pity I have for them
To see you and not know
To hear you speak and yet, not hear
You are my one and only
Another couldn't come close to half your value

Precious Name

I spoke to you
Never expecting you to answer
But you did
I was so amazed and filled with joy
I screamed and
Laughed out loud
A joy released from you went through my fingers
And colored the air
Suddenly, trees had endless roots
And birds flew through sky and space
Rain fell not from clouds but from hearts
The earth wasn't our toil
But our glory
Everything got brighter; lighter
And time stood still for me
For you,
You spoke to me
When I called your name
And I've been calling it ever since
Jade.

When Sisi calls

It starts with a damp cloth
Cotton fibers purposed and poised
Dancing around open wounds strategically hidden
Hidden from eyes, hidden with ties
Strings dangling from my weary heart
These fibers dance with delicacy and grace
They tend wounds this world could never imagine
Of the pain that never was but will be
The tears that pour and choke me
The fear that creeps in slow and deep
Waltzes to its own consuming beat
These wounds, these fibers dress
She listens with every mop of liquid
Measures my words spoken and implied
She's never tried to change who I am
But instead help me be
One word at a time
One hug at a time
The hug you feel through wireless connections
Hug with prayers that thwart the enemy's deception
For her words are rooted in her God
Our God
Mine
She reminds me of His love, His presence, His grace
She holds mirrors high to show me salivation's restoring face
When sisi calls
Its surgery, then stitches
Pointy metal piercing my flesh, my heart
A perfect hem for loose thoughts
Seeping brokenness and despair

Thoughts that wound me deeper
That cut and tear
Tear me from the faith I know I have
And pull me from the God I know I believe in
The God I trust with my sustenance and healing
The God who always was
And will always be
The God who created, and truly knows me
Whose plan for me is perfect …
Whose mercy to me is kind …
The God who speaks to me
Whenever my sisi calls

For You

If my heart was big enough
I'd make a banner out of it
And hang your name in letters of gold
If I could plant a heart in the soil
I'd grow diamonds of you everywhere
Still –
I believe,
They can't handle this much genius
They can't manage this much pure
They would become greedy and destructive
They would waste all your good
And the world would lose itself
In the vastness of your worth

Odes of Correction

She sits him on her lap
Locks her hand against his back
Supports his posture and interpretation
For she is about to teach
And he knows
He lifts his chin and turn his eyes to meet her gaze
Closes his lips to feed on her words with his heart
Each word is a candle lit
A fiery glare he will remember years from now
But she isn't harsh
For he is young and new
Still, she is instructive just the same
She holds his hands and transfers all her hope to him
She is sure...
He will be better than us
He must
And in that moment of correction
I see my sister mother
And I know
Somehow
My nephew understands

Ichigo

My heart breaks with your melancholy
When you shut the doors inside and out
And bottle with classic tunes
Inviting snow in June
When the hurricanes of your emotions rage on
And I cannot help
I breakaway
You never bring us close to your valley
Never leave a trail of breadcrumbs to guide us to your place of retreat
When you go, you hide
In perfect plain view
And we can only sniff for a whiff
Reach into the air for a clue
But you
How we love and cherish you
How I know you are the best of all of us
But I can never tell you
I can never share
The depths of my indebtedness
And how much I care
My heart breaks
Every time melancholy rings at your door
And you let her in
And leave us outside

Lessons

I could cry more tears if you close your eyes
I could break apart at each rugged edge if you turn away,
But when I see your face I stop and convince myself
I must be strong for you in this moment.
I must be who you've taught me to be.

Happiness is

Happiness is
Her eyes
The wonder behind lids closed in perfect peace
For now
As she sleeps
When tomorrow comes she'll be busy building vocabulary and faith
She will know her mother's God
The God of her father and her grandparents
She will pray like they have prayed before
And more
Those eyes will pour anointing over her Master's feet in worship
And with thanksgiving
Happiness is...
Her eyes

Playing with colors

Ten fingers play with the colors of my heart
They never paint me mad
Only shades of wonder
They give me tones of awe and amazement
Lines of unsure
And splashes of fear
But they never leave me bare
I have ten fingers playing with the colors of my heart

Two eyes color me willing
Wanting to wrap the best of the world and give it away
They border me with limitlessness
Of love
And mix me with forgiveness and hope
Wisdom is sketched in the pattern
Understanding birthed on the page as a lantern
Lessons I will learn shaped on the tip of the brush

One miracle paints me tomorrow
An image brightened with hope
A canvas is redeemed
New purpose hangs itself in the world's museum
Owning its space on the wall
The work praises the worker
The painted pays homage to the painter
This
For ever choosing to play with the colors of my heart

Precious...

The picture not taken the one behind the lens will always remember
The warm wind that saved a life no hymn will know in December
The autumn leaf that fell that was the dearest to the tree
The love I know will never grow but will forever be

The smile in a crowd a single eye only did behold
The precious stone the Builder saved to be His treasured gold
We will long for you more hours than the day could ever provide
The pain, I know, will dissipate but the love will never subside.

Mercy

This is for that rose you might pass in the corner
Standing solid in her own little space
She is
Bold enough to be beautiful
And yet
Broken enough to shed petals
You might see her dancing by the window's ledge
Testing the sun for what it's worth
She's not afraid to push beyond the expected
And fight for her right to speak
Listen
You can learn from her
As I have

Birdie

Be there a heart that's like summer
And eyes as deep as the sea
If a fellow was like a crayon box
Then that's what my birdie would be
With red for his bright love
And purple, his personality
Green his inspiring embrace
And black his ethereal solidity
Be there a wave to carry you across a mountain
Or a leap across a field
So my birdie's smile could empower a nation
And his truth be their shield
Dear Lord, shine Your love on him like summer
Enlarge his territory as wide as the sea
Safeguard his heart as Your treasured music box
For this is how much my birdie means to me

Typical

He has his ways and you have yours
It's easy to chastise him for his mistakes
His chronic shortcomings that often frustrate
But that's all good and well for now
Drop the shade to the looking glass and turn –
There's the mirror
What? –
No darts left to throw?
No stone left to fling?
Why is there no more wielding of the sword?
Has your arm grown hypocritical too?
Following your mind down that popular path?
He does his bad, leave him be
But don't you judge him!
He's done less than you
I mean, me.

Anachronistic Naivety

I have considered the possibility
That I might have thrived more effortlessly
In the welcoming arms of a time earlier than now.
This, of course measured in my mind
As a plausible explanation for my affinity to ancient things;
Culture and poise
Art and revolution.
Some say I am far too motherly when I speak
For a wee lass my age
And that my opinions, with regard to contemporary inclinations,
Disprove any validity of my appreciation for
Youth and children alike.
Naturally, I do not subscribe to such conclusions,
Though it does make one pause to think:
Which era would I most like to go back to?
(If such a thing were even a possibility in the slightest)
In what time could I both thoroughly enjoy the authentic novelty of
the day
And yet flourish amidst the vicissitudes that so frequently follow revival?
I ponder such things
And will confess, I find it entertaining so to do

Until I walk into a room and see my niece looking back at me
With eyes purposed; her version of her mother's stare,
Or hear my nephew practicing the alphabet
And saying 'no!', like only he can.
I ponder until I consider my brother and sister;
There is no guarantee that I would have the same siblings as I do now –
Such a prospect is complete horror in its own way!
My daddy would not be my daddy,

The friends dear to my heart now
Would not be in my life
I would miss the pleasures of sitting in at dance rehearsals
Or hear my darlings improvise through drama for the next day
And the homes I steal into on days I feel lost
Would not have been built yet!
The four walls I pin my fears to at the edge of Linstead
Would not host the same souls it does today
And I would be just me
In all my might or glee maybe -
But without them

I ponder my fixation on other eras
But then I forget all that babble
In light of all the things that make this time
Remarkable
And I play cords on the strings of my pen
Singing about the extraordinary joy
Of living now

Home

These are the faces I know
Curves and blemishes that have taught me love

These are the hands I know
Palms that have offered me warmth

These are the voices I know
Sounds that have given me hope

These are the tears that I know
Pain that disarms me like nothing else

These are the ones I love
Love that has given me peace

These are them who are my blood
The best parts of me extended from a being undeserving

These are they who have been my place
My favorite place

Home

People say,
"You are going to live long,
I just called your name!"

I prefer to think it means I will
survive on the lips of those who love me
even after I am gone…

The World and I

Echoes & Silence

Throat is empty
Cheeks heavily salted
Walk in a room with no colors
Count the strokes of the times you've faulted
And faltered
Where's the dustpan to sweep away the ashes?
Get rid of the evidence of fire
Would you dare to rise like a phoenix?
Turn the mockers into liars?
They conspired
Against you and all you believe
Surprise them with lungs expanded and tightened
Let them watch wonder unfold
In your echoes and silence
A paradox undivided
A kindness unrequited
Let them witness your soul unfold
In your echoes and silence

Troubadour

(For Maya and the others..)

Whose words can lift a mountain and plant a seed under it?
When the leaves find their freedom through hot, melted earth,
Who are you who sees it?
She colors the air with her breath
And he shields a hope with his words
When an ocean hugs the feet of a child at play
And the hem of her dress is carried through time
Who is he that makes the words a thousand and one?
Who are you who reads them?
You are the passenger on a journey unrestricted
The interpreter of a language undefined
Her beating heart is your inspiration
And his thoughts the pillow on which you dream
Whose words can lift a mountain and plant a seed under it?
With every stanza the tree grows
It will root itself in today
And then, -
Build a world tomorrow

Brick

Amazing what heat can do -
Leave a heart in the fire
Bare a soul to the flames
Stitch hope to a melting faith
How much more then we pay attention
How then,
Little by little,
Clay becomes brick
And brick becomes steel.

Run

Take a step out the door
Push yourself further than you ever did before
Keep your eyes fixed – listen for the gun
Quiet your heart in that moment
and then,
Run!
There is nothing that can limit you
Nothing to make what's plenty, few
Only you can keep your head from the shining sun
So don't complain about the rain
Just run!
Power through these dark moments
Push past whatever makes you too tense
Shake the chains off your feet –
The race has begun
Don't worry about the finish line
Just run!

T R U T H

Truth for you, dear girl;
Truth for you to find.
Truth to anchor tomorrow;
Truth to wisdom bind.
Truth to be bare -
Truth to open your heart,
Truth to face the consequences -
Truth to own your part.
Truth in the eyes of a babe,
Truth on the cheeks of a flower;
Truth to multiply among the masses,
Truth religiosity can't devour.
Truth in Government halls.
Truth on scholarly specs.
Truth for a child to hear -
Truth no father should forget.
Truth I want to know,
Truth I want to share;
Truth to help me be better,
Truth to fight my fear.

Killing Conversation

We've killed conversation, haven't we?
Taking beautiful phrases and shrinking them in the wash
Adding too much nothing for the sake of being brief
Rinsing with letters instead of complete words
Hanging them out to dry
To die
On paper and with our voice
Who stabbed Good Morning? I can't decipher GM
Who poisoned okay? Keep your potassium,
K?
Resuscitate courtesies will you, please!
Doctor of pleasantries, revive love in expression!
Give breath again to words that encourage!
In their entirety
Respect the sobriety
And, Dear Sir, grant me a kindness
Uncaringly awake inspiration in speech
There is much more to beseech
But if nothing else, grant me this:
Enough words that can give me the strength to resist
And not load another sentence in the machine I just bought

Time

To never have enough of you brings frequent tears
To have too much of you
Well,
That has its own problems too

Everyone wants you in *their* ideal amount
We take for granted that you are a child we can all boss around
We want you to slow down at our chosen leisure
We want you to hurry away to bring us closer to pleasure
We pat you on the head then seat you in the corner
We beckon you to our side when it is in our favor

I won't ask you for yesterday anymore
Or bombard you with foolish enquiries about tomorrow
There is little good that will do for me
The focus is to try and live here
Now

Hill Climb

No mountain is endless
Only some steeper than others

When forgiveness is offered and not requested
When faith fights and survives whenever it is tested
When honesty is freely and openly poured out
And the tongue can be subdued by the doors of the mouth
When hope is kept alive and shared with everyman
When high horses are abandoned and on one level we stand
When houses have warmth and homes are reborn
When we learn to stitch each other's garments after they've been torn
When we can turn to the morning sun and see the beauty in a day
And learn that the little things get their value from the pleasantries we say
When we meet fear with boldness and triumph with humility
When we can eradicate synthetic 'empathetic' duplicity
When we commit to believing and dreaming again
And we can trust in the finality of a resounding "Amen"
It will mean the same for students, mothers, preachers and scholars
That no mountain is endless
Only some steeper than others

If

If when you worry
The odds change in your favor
And time is added to your lot,
Then,
Worry away.

If when you opt for the negative
You prosper in your pursuits
And advance in all your duties,
Then,
Be sour all the day.

If by your unkindness
You are swept into contentment
And you finally experience peace,
Then,
By all means,
Be mean.

But if you are paused at any time,
In a moment of being kind-
If ever you merry meet,
In a moment of being sweet,
Fall prey to those habits, I bid you;
Make practice of the seldom tried.

For if at any time you'd rather step outside of your head,
And put to better use anything on which worry might be fed,
Then take a pen and walk with me out here-
Take a pen and write with me out here.

Perhaps

Perhaps
You are here because it is an anomaly
You are attracted to it simply because it is an oddity
A counter-concept to the masses;
The recipient of your great disdain and ire
You find comfort here
(In a loose sense of the word)
Because you must explain and defend
Stand clad in armor for the battle of enquiry
This is acceptable to you
For in this
You find purpose
And who doesn't want to have that?

Under Dirt & Stone

I bury my imperfections
Hide them away from scrutinizing eyes
And unkind lips that do nothing but criticize
I force them under dirt and stone
And keep them from those mirrors on the street
That have been built to reflect a different standard of beauty –
The silly, manmade, synthetic kind –
That time and time again triggers doubt in mind
About my beauty
About the preciousness of my skin
But this has nothing to do with color
This is about the unsequenced potential that lives within me
The uncontained passion that tries so hard to break free
This is about my word choice and how, sometimes, I play it safe
Because I don't want to offend or seem too brazen
This is about the times when I don't care and I just write anyway
This is about how much of an introvert I am which causes others to think
I'm depressed
This is about the undiscovered quality of the way I love that average hearts
would describe as being obsessed
This is about my insufficiencies
That apparently quantify me as a human being
And for this reason, I must be fixed –
Enter the handymen and women with their tools –
This is about me starting to think I may be broken indeed
Or simply weird
Or just misunderstood
Maybe all of it
I Don't know anymore
So,

I bury the excess of me I no longer wish to have people abuse
To be honest, I've taken some of the core parts of me too
Left it under rubble to decay and fade away
I'm hoping though that one day, before long
I will realize that treasures are buried too
But they were never meant to be kept under soil or rock
They deserve to be dug up, dusted and admired
For the priceless and extraordinary value they possess.

Conflict

Howsoever I am able to stand before thee,
Perhaps as weary waves cling to flirting shores;
May I offer a trembling, parting reprise-
And be restless with myself no more.

For many years I have wrestled with my fear-
One score, six and some;
Forget I a time when courage would battle for me,
And leave with me thrill and wisdom.

These days are different, I must confess,
My own defense has found to be lacking still;
Though I have tried to battle as I did from old,
This fear will not bend to my will.

It stood against me as a boasting Philistine,
Solid, stubborn and strong-
Failed, my efforts did, to knock down this opposer
And cast it hence to where it belongs.

I rallied and wrought and clamored at length,
Spending and trading and wasting my strength-
Hitherto I knew only my own feeble defense,
Now I am left wanting, bruised and indifferent.

My pulse has slowed and my fervor drained;
Silence has dressed me as a footman heavy with melancholy-
I drag my heel henceforward like thee
Knew I not the seed nor blossomed deed of my folly.

Complexus Poetria

Lost in the wreckage
Tiptoeing around the destruction
Bandages and rugs stacked high
Carpets hiding shame
The depths of these rivers have no treading torsos
No evidence of tracks on the stony floor
Count yourself lucky to have made it this far
To know this much
If luck was a great misfortune
An invitation to the curious and unfortunate
To be burdened without realizing
Line by line
To be pinched with sadness
Word by word
To miss what you have not lost
To hope for what was never meant to be yours
To head in a direction unadvised
To inquire and to wonder
To try and understand a great complexity;
The chaos of my reverie

How to save a life

Had I known how exactly to
The fray would be more deliberate
My sighs more calculated
An actually accurate filter to words thought of and written
Syllables, puns and conundrums
Plastered on paper for strangers' eyes to abuse
Unconquered emotions unsure what pen to choose
Or which lines to lose
Sifting through words that tease
Words left light in the wind on white trees dead from human hands
Dying again at my own
Truth that tempts through punctuation marks
And frightens with every stanza
Still, these lyrics have been the constant death of my insecurities
A lynching of the suppositions of my inadequacies
Every title is a press against a chest once thought still
Each metaphor a breath replaced in deprived vessels
A dare to look and hear
To taste and imagine with this graphite
To feel, if I must
And understand the immense risk that comes with it
To close my eyes and hope they rise
These words, flying above rejection and grief
Outlasting praise and applause
By living, day by day
In hearts yet to be formed
To shape lives yet to be given birth to
And through this
Moment by moment
Giving me
A pulse

It's been a while

You took me back to thirteen
Proud and with reason
Just enough to be level-headed and interested
You took me back to Creed and Bon Jovi
Staind
To Rick D's and Waterhouse
To trips in places the new mind has forgotten but that the heart still tastes
I traveled to new discoveries and you guided me
We drank wine and laughed with folly
Now folly is not as jovial
Where will you take me next?
What else shall I discover?
You took me back to tummy laughs
And pranks and jokes
To tomorrow and yesterday
To the straight path… to the abandoned way
You took me back to phone calls of disappointment
And slaps with straps
And redemption with the dew
You took me back … You take me now
Where will you take me next?
What else shall I discover?

Inadequate

Feels like baskets unable to carry sunshine
Or smile unable to touch the heart
Empties like canals without a stream
A hem without a seam
A vineyard with sticks in the mud
Waiting for the threads of life to dance about them

It -
Advances like ambition without character
Rises with reward and honor not gained
It nods without esteem
Makes currency of broken dreams
Sits on the high of a hill of regret
Swallowing the emotions of a soul hung low

It –
Loves without truth
Hugs without the warmth
Always knows there is more
Will never admit that it is sure
For who wants to be reminded everyday
That inadequate is the only word of me that I can say

Journey

On every path leading to somewhere special
These footprints leave a deeper trail
I stop more, waiting and wondering
Second guessing the next pull off muscle
The next crash of will into dirt
Waiting, wondering, hoping to see
If I will ever make it to where I'm supposed to go

Mirror of a Beauty

I saw your beauty.
It was a dancing lad on paved streets of white untrusting lines and yellow markings of caution and timidity.
Above the harsh asphalt it beckoned to me with a voice not that of a wailing woman but one of a babe shivering from cold.
Your beauty is an injustice;
A hallow reminder of things hoped for and not received and things expected but deprived of.
Your reflection is your own disdain.
Sad.
You are so beautiful.
You are the curve of letters formed on papers by poets.
You are the envy of musicians and preachers;
The hunted by those appraised and often times thoughtlessly adored;
The dream of anxious fingers and toes developing;
The song of birds behind bars;
The whisper of the moon and the humming of the sun.
Your fantasy fantasies about you…
Your face, your arms
Your beauty.
Yes, I saw your beauty,
Not with my eyes but with my heart,
Enveloping me with your honesty and challenging me with your plea for care.
I approach –
Guarded against your perceived endlessness
But embracing of your potential.
You warn me that the lines of your palm are a map for treasures imagined,
Hidden beyond slippery terrain

And that the dip of your chin is a tale of bitter sweet endings for heeding proverbs
Your large commanding eyes reflect a hazel enticement; still your mouth offers prudence.
I am bemused.
Your frolic waves a warning red.
Will they see it?
I see your beauty, Free.
I see your beauty,
Not with my eyes but with my heart.

Evidence of Rain

There's a smile on the hill
Making its way home
The first sign was a chill
And then the sweep of wind through the hair like comb

Tiny skin sprouts populate and decorate
Jackets and coats give tighter embrace
Cotton hung in the sky spells out the coming fate
A single lost lad makes a land on the face

"There is evidence of rain", she said
With soaked cheeks dripping
"Never mind, don't worry", she said
"Dry your tears with singing"

All Through His 'Him'

She broke her back for him every time he ached
Smeared her cheeks with dust and dirt –
Everything but pride and pain covered her face
She did it because she thought he deserved the best
Never mind her own slim figure –
It was him that deserved the best dress
Don't think she was a woman without esteem
Going all through his him
She was just a woman lost
In the cloud of her own altruism

From A Glass Window

I watched him
From the convenience of my glass window and wooden seat
He had a chair of his own;
A permanent essential he could barely survive without.
I saw her push him by;
His eyes lost without focus, but bright -
And I wondered, for a second,
What he saw and what he felt.
Did he recognize this world?
Which parts of the little things laying around did he make sense of?
Then I thought,
How different am I from this man in his wheelchair?
How much of this world did I ever stop long enough to make sense of?
I pondered the possibility that I had lived this life like a dream,
Waiting for the next character to appear
For the next sequence of events to unfold
Never deliberate enough about love or potential;
Never bold enough to dance with the particles in the air;
To dare to be more than just a user of machine.
He went by and, somehow, I know, if he could,
He would dance on the pavement beneath his feet.
He would sing the notes of songs he loved to the joy of those who loved him
And to the annoyance of those who were too rigid to understand.
Then, a tear came to my eye
Not because I felt sorry for him, but because I felt sorry for me.
I wanted to dance and ignite the particles all around me!
Perhaps I could have, if I got out of my seat –
But I remained seated in my wooden chair,
And went back to my machine.

Boxes in the attic

There are boxes in the attic I haven't touched
I've cleaned the top and bottom floors
Emptied the half-filled glasses
And dumped the excess food down the sink
I vacuumed the carpet and dusted my window blades
I've done a decent enough job, I think
But those boxes, I have avoided
I have no use for them anyways
Let them gather dust and waste away in the dark
Let their contents expire from no attention at all

New

Forget the ash of a day burnt.
When the grey of opportunities stare back at you,
Heap it at the roots of chances yet to bloom.
That lily petal that slipped through your fingers;
The one that lost itself in the wind,
Wish it well – It will serve another good.
You'd never stop to imagine that the raindrops that assaulted your laundry
Brought joy to a man brown from thirst
Or parched cattle grazing in the field.
What you curse, another praises.
What brings you wrath may very well be someone else's peace.

Preserve your tears for occasions that demand it.
Spend not your energy on things already gone.
Give every day a fighting chance.
Stop, when you must -
Rest, if you have to.
Love anew
Hope anew;
Summon your courage for these things.

Then, watch the freshness of a soft hello
Wipe clear the memories of those harsh goodbyes.

At My Invitation (Part I)

Forgive me if I'm not angry enough in everything I write
Or that all my stanzas aren't explosive enough for you
That you don't see 'power' in some of the words I use
The funny thing about it all is that this is my poetry
And I get to decide which words I choose
This is my pen, not yours
I've fallen prey to your expectations one too many times
In so many different areas of my life
But not this time
Not with this
This is a thousand percent me
And what I see and what I feel
You have no authority here
You are privileged to sit and be served my inner thoughts
To taste the flavor of my curiosity and thrill
To salivate at the marinade of my desires and pain exciting your senses
Here, you are given
You do not demand nor solicit
This is my pen
My best friend
You are a guest
And you are seated
At my invitation alone

Without being lost,
Find yourself in the midst of this great big world -
Find yourself in spite of this great big world.

God & I

Love Note

Is it possible to even serenade You,
You who are word itself?
If I could write symphonies and compose brilliant lines of music
Would it be enough to describe how You make me feel –
You who are song itself?
You are brilliance manifested
And immaculate in every aspect
How could I write a love poem for You
When You are love
Perfect love alone?

In Response to Your Invitations (Part II)

You see, I know what it is you wanted to say
But haven't you exaggerated a 'bit' in your issuing of invitations?
Shall I receive one too?
Am I on your list of invitees?
Will I be given an RSVP stub to reserve My seat at your grand feast?
Tell me, dear chef and host
Who gave you the produce to fiddle with?
The seasonings and spices you toss around, who placed them in your reach?
The recipes that you cook up,
Who gave you the inspiration to be bold enough to mix words the way
you do?
I entreat you my dear,
For I Am is your humble guest,
May I sit?
Wont you allow Me to partake of your masterpiece?
Your grand creation that is a 'thousand percent you'?
And here I thought I gave you ink and page
Opened your mind and whispered to your senses
But I see my darling
This is all you
I am merely your guest
So,
If you so please,
Entertain Me
Entertain us all

Beautiful

Have you seen it;
The beauty of a mountain giving way to a river to run free?
Or the smooch of the sky and clouds by a sea otherwise pale?

Have you heard how tree roots and soil reason together,
And how leaves clap their hands at the symphonies of feathers composing music?

Perhaps you have tasted the flavors of wind and rain
Seated at a culinary table unmatched, feasting with Earth itself.
Have you?

Have you ever stopped to feel how new eyes tend to pierce the soul
And that there is nothing quite equal to when those ten fingers hold on to trembling cheeks
Because that way, they truly see you and that touch,
Has made you known?

Isn't it amazing that all of this starts and ends with You, Elohim?
Isn't it spectacular that they are templates of Your design?
What a wonderful thing!
A wonderfully beautiful thing indeed!

Ode

The freshest spring on the hottest day
Quenching the thirst of all who come –
Thirsts for You.
You are the love song whispered by the trees to the sun
A silent, glorious serenade unique to every leaf;
Every branch.
Oh! that we would be silent with You
And live a life always proclaiming Your Glory!
My God, the hope found in a morning
And the rest which evening provides,
You are magnificent in all Your creation
Matchless, indomitable in all Your works!

Do I

Do I
Yearn for you because your presence is my filling?
Do I
Crave your touch because your embrace is my ceiling
My endless, unmistakable high?
Do I
Long to hear you speak because your words are the reason my skin dances
upon itself
And reveals how inspiration is painted upon pores
Once unsure
But now
Wholly captivated
Completely still
Do I
Need you
Because breath and life
Living and living
Are cushioned in your bosom
Cradled in the warmth of the breadth of your chest
My peace place
Do I
Sacrifice to you because then my worship is made complete?
So sweet
The incense of a heart laid on the alter
Set ablaze with selflessness
Consumed through contrition
Kindled by Brokenness
Do I
Yield to your will because you taught me so in practice

Demonstrated how to live a life faithful and that this
World is just a passing phase
Time organized in passing days
That the real reason we do, the real reason we are, the reason we can
Is purely because of the I Am
And that nothing else compares
Whatever compels
Thy word have I hid in my heart
To dispel
All that would pull me away from you
You, Lord
Do I
Love you because you have shown me love
Do I
Stand in awe of you because of what you have done
Sending your son
A sacrifice for me?
This unworthy?
This unclean?
Do I
Do
Enough for you?
Not yet
Never will
But help me be still
Keep me in gaze of your glory
Forever reverent to your holy
Paused by the utterings of your spirit
Charged to go by the conviction of the salvation you have gifted me
Take me, take us
For nothing else can ever be enough
Make us
Your living sacrifices

Storyteller

I know I have been distant
I try folding myself within the pages of my flesh
Foolishly daring to sink deeper into that persistent, unambiguous sensation
That I have wandered away from You
I cannot look You in the eyes of Your Word
Could never stand in Your presence of worship
Nor seek refuge in the midst of Your people
No, I have positioned myself at the back end of this shelf
Wallowing in my manmade detachment –
As if I could ever hide from You
Still, You make Your way around and find me
Open these hard covers I've worked hard to cover
And continue to pen Your great masterpiece
And I cannot understand how You still make use of me
How You enter the leaves of this scrapped book
And manage to fill these empty lines with joy
You have transcribed a love language on sheets worn and withered
That has not been fathomed, that has not been praised to the heights of
praising
Nor revered to the vastness which reverence demands
You have taken up this empty thing
Traded the innocence of Your Kin
And offered me a story
Gave me a plot, setting and climax of my own
Expertly orchestrated the flow of characters
Inserted in seasons and at points brilliantly timed
You have written purpose upon this life
Gifted me with wonder and awe standing in the presence of Your glorious
exhale;
God-breathed, God's deed, God's desire to have me live

Not die –
To declare Your works great!
Not shy away from my purpose;
The reason You created me in the first place
The reason You still write upon these withered, worn out pages
Infusing within the context of this narrative
The Gospel of Jesus Christ;
How He has never left me
Not even to my own destructive, wayward devices
And how He doesn't intend to

The Woman & The Prophet

She could have buried herself under the pain of a promise now dead
But she wasn't in the habit of digging graves
She could have told her husband and a servant the truth
But she wasn't in the habit of baring her heart for others to see
Only to a prophet who walked in her life
Only to a prophet she let lay in her house
Only to a prophet who could not help but bless her
Only with a blessing for which she did not ask
"Shunamite woman, is it well with your husband?
Shunamite woman is it well with your son?
Shunamite woman is it well with you?
Shunamite woman, what would you have me do?"
"Give me back the promise you made
Prophet, restore the boy to me which you gave
Go yourself, he is in your room
This Shunamite woman will build no tomb!"
She could have cried herself hopeless in the streets
But she wasn't a hopeless mourner
She could have sent for help instead of a donkey
But she had no need for a coroner
Shunamite woman, your promise has come back to thee
Shunamite woman, his flesh has known again heat
Shunamite woman, knowest thou what other needs?
Nothing more for this Shunamite woman
She has heard her promise sneeze

Mary of Magdala

My name shall they commune with harlotry
My reputation shalt many despise
My story shall they skew in bias
My affliction only, shall many reprise

But I have seen the Savior
I have wept at His feet
How much more my story shalt change
If ever in glory we meet

The pain in my life is true
My torment I could never deny
But release I met in the form of a Nazarene
Who is called Jesus the Christ

Anarchy

And if the sky was to posture in defiance
Arguing that it would much rather be the earth
For it feels that hanging high is not it's calling
And it was made to eventually come to this conclusion -
If it goes on to take its place beneath the clouds
And abandons its position in creation
To take stature created from its folly,
Shall the rest of Earth not witness this and respond?
Shan't the Mother of Nature itself beckon to it and say,
Be not deceived?
And if, while below, this sky repositioned, reasoned with rootless trees
Seeking depth in sand, stone or sea
To hence concoct an idea to refashion the design of Nature's gowns
To rebrand her garments and offer her newer, more expansive choices -
If, after sometime, she acquiesces and actually joins in their exploits,
Shall the truth vanish with their respect for reverence and restraint?
Will it still not remain,
Be not deceived?
And if sky repositioned and trees rootless triumphed in getting ocean and
mountain to join their cause
And animal alike took its place in this radical quest -
If there were no boulders nor pebbles,
No flower nor raging forest that stood in opposition;
If this decision taken by one, to challenge everything breathed from
Genesis,
Facilitates the claim of independent identity for all created
And all that was previously considered to be
Rests in the wreckage of any attribute to a 'sort-of-god'

And irreverent anarchy among the created creates the illusion of
intelligence –
Will not this endeavor lead to one inevitable end?
Won't a single thought confound all that 'glorious' progress?
And isn't that singular thought not this:
Be not deceived, God is not mocked?

You are God

When the sun shines
You are God
When the rain pours
You are God
If the mountains should fall into the sea tomorrow
You are God
If the streams never should run dry
You are God
When my hands are lifted high in praise
You are God
If they should wrap my belly in pain
You are God
When my bucket is running over
You are God
When my cup is turned down and dry
You are God
When I laugh with joy
You are God
If only all I do is cry
You are God
When the wars rage
You are God
When peace rains
You are God
Through sickness and despair
You are God
When grief draws near
You are God
When the tears old become new
You are God

When condolences won't do
You are God
When I succeed on the first try
You are God
When I fail miserably, time and again
You are God
If the sky should bleed in the morning
You are God
If it should be blue until your Kingdom comes here on Earth
You are God
Whether we sing of Your Glory
Or mock our own selves with conceit
You are God
If we bring you burnt offerings
You are God
If sticks and stones replace us in a breath
You are God
Whether the store houses be full
Or the barns remain empty
Even if the trees bear no fruit
High or low, happy or sad
You are God
Bless your name
Forever and ever
For you are God!

Haphazard

Haphazard
A suited mannequin of disorder
Synthetic and only for show
Uncultured
Untamed
Weary
Tired from aimlessness
Wretchedly exhausted from uncertainty
Worried
Wrestles
Doubtful
Distracted
Diffident
Each breath skeptic
Without assurance or faith
Panicked
Pestered
Pessimistic
Woe is everything!
Pained
Trying to find meaning
Lost
Lonely
Less interested in surviving
Floating
Drifting
Barely getting by
Trapped by the void of sin and separation
Floating
Drifting by with

No direction
Without You

But
Conversely
However

I am
Anchored
Guided
Pulled with purpose towards You
Drawn to the fullness of life because of You
Mercy leads me towards You
Grace ushers me to Your arms
Your peace has given me focus
Your love has given me gravity
And my God!
By God!
That gravity
Has kept me
Grounded

Learning Still

How can I compromise your standards?
Trade my gift of sonship for a bastard's?
Refuse the union of mercy and grace
And flaunt disobedience in your face?
How can I betray your perfect complete love
And hide from the Peace created above?
How could I give more value to the words they say?
With their ignorant pomposity and misguided ways?
When was the moment exact
When life started to demand from me substandard scraps?
When I give only a portion of me
A part of who I was created to be?
A half felt shout
Maybe, kinda praises from my mouth
O silly me in my folly
Traded salvation for monopoly
Exchanged righteousness for an idler's fee
Consumed with destructive fleshly glee
Oh silly me!
Let it not be silly you!
Learn from my mistakes
Turn your eye from the fruit's sweet taste
The appeal, the pull
Christ already paid the price in full
Do not let his offering be in vain
He suffered, bled and died,
What pain!
Forgive us, Your children, Lord I cry
We turn our heart and eyes to You,
Only You, on high.

Trusting You

Lord, my faults are many
What can be counted for me is few
But I am giving tomorrow away
And trusting it to You
The fears are plenty
And the doubt settles like dew
But I'm giving you my circumstance
And trusting it to You
My family needs my attention
And though my love for them is true
I am tired and weary Lord
So I'm trusting them to You
There are many plans in place Oh God
So many dreams set on queue
But lest I make a mess of me oh Father
I'm trusting them to You
Provide, sustain and heal you will
Thy grace unmerited but due
Help me leave it all in Your hands
And trust all of me to You

Tears of Rain

You cried with me didn't You?
Heart of my heart, You felt the quake
Held on to the pieces
And poured Yourself into the cracks
When reality struck
Slithered its way around my unguarded hope
Tightened its muscles
Causing me a pain I have never known
Lunging its fangs at my faith
Cutting off my air,
You gave me release
Sweet breath for me to breathe
There was sunshine again
How ironic –
In the rain I saw the most beautiful of suns
In the rain I felt the warmest stroke of its rays on my face
And with the tears You cried for my pain,
The Earth drank in Your expression of Love
I smiled – relaxed my muscles and basked in that glorious moment
The moment my God cried for me
So I didn't have to cry anymore.

Treats

He dropped tiny bars of happiness in the pockets of my coat —
Two on each side to get me started on my day
I was almost out of supply when during break
I found bite-sizes of faith to nibble on at lunch

He does this to me often;
Sneak me sweet surprises to flavor my journey

I know I don't deserve them
And I know He knows too
But He keeps on giving me treats —
Like assurance in decorative boxes
And hope in gold plastic wraps twisted at both ends

He always gives me enough to share
He doesn't expect me to eat all my treats alone

Rest

Who among you is restless?
Find peace in the arms of the King
His arms - whose comfort is comparable to none
For a thousand beds of cotton significantly fall short
And simply become undone

Mind Games

Supposing the mind gave a whiff
Would its aura in air be a fragrance or a stench?
Would it have danced on the petals of a flower sweet or rise from a roaring trench?

Consider thoughts a TV overhead.
What would your actors depict on screen?
Would the plot played out for the world claim worth in being seen?

What if the mind were to mix a concoction.
Would yours bear the brand of elixir quickly?
Or a dollar buy over counter to get them dazed and tipsy?

For whatever is pure, train the mind thus:
Be pleasing in secret and admirable in the sun.
Keep the reins on in secret to bring honor to the Son.

For You Have Made It So

For You have made it so
Gift wrapped packages of moments
That we've lost in the wrapping of time
Wrapped hearts, rapt hearts
Rapping
"Let's share!
Hold me
Near!
Pulse, blood, hands;
Something I can see!
I want to be Yours
But his too!
Hers too!"
It hurts You
But You give us moments.
We've lost days to pursuits for prosperity
Pardoned your plans for pagan planet posterity
Building like those early folk hoping to reach heaven
Thinking the clouds are too high up
So we rather physically rise up
Than to gain growth points for righteous
Landing on the right side of pious
And against the enemy size up
This fight's us
Versus them
But best believe if the inner You ain't Him
Stay off the battle field

And Sweeter Still

Refrain

How much sweeter can You get?

How much more loving can You be?

How much more righteous, glorious and gracious is Thee?

Just How more beautiful?

Is there still more to come?

Lord I salute You, 'cause Yuh praises caa done..

Verse 1

I remember when I cried unto You from my wilderness

Beseeched Thee to take me out of my mess

I begged You Lord, and You gave me my deliverance

You raised me up in the light of Your countenance

Lord, I basked in Your glory all filled

Feeling Holy and sanctified, but yet still

You were working things out, still giving me your sugar

I have divine diabetes; You're my soul's great lover

Now I worship from the mountaintop and ask

While I praise You, 'cause it's my life's great task.....

Just how much sweeter can You get?

Verse 2

Lord, my God, the exhibition of great:

You define faithfulness, so in you I put my faith

God, Abba Father, the Bright Morning Star,

You are the drier of tears and the healer of scars

El Shadi, Jehovah Rapha, Jehovah Nisi,

Creator God, my deliverer, the lily of the valley

My King, my lawyer, my brother and my friend
I will love You Lord, 'till my life shall end

While I try to grasp how could You love me so
How is it You fill me up 'till my banks overflow
I will surrender my life to You ;
Your praises are in my mouth
I will live my life with You just trying to figure out....

How much sweeter can You get?

Verse 3
Everything is for a time and season, that's what Your Word says
Nothing will last forever; it must come to an end
So I don't expect to be on this hilltop always
My valley must come again.....one day
The trials will come to teach me what they have to
Lord just prepare me to stand firm in battle
In all things give thanks; that's what You require
Help me in the wilderness to fulfill this desire
And there also Lord, even through any tears
Let me remember this verse to get me past all fears

Sadness & Grief

Approach of Death

How does death come?
Does it come like a whisper in the ear?
Does it waltz to our doom as it draws near?
Will it come like the silver steel of life's regret?
Fired in the hearts of the ones we wish could forget?
Is it like the roar of a lion in the jungle?
Does it grumble?
Is it like feather to the palm or cotton to the skin?
Will it sting like hot metal when our end begins?
Does it pinch the soul?
Makes the coward bold?
Are there words to give final peace?
A secret moment of preparation for final release?
Does it laugh or wear a dismal face?
Will it hold the hand it takes to meet his fate?
How does death come?
May that be answered at its appointed time.

To Be Mother

The kick isn't there today
No turning in the tummy anymore
Fingers framed only on a black and white screen
No head against the birthing door

Three seconds she had
Or three hundred years, maybe
I've never known the pain she feels
I know no prescription, no remedy

Remember the women who were mothers for a minute
Who in womb, held their hope
The ones who've cried a thousand tears
The ones left inventing ways to cope

This one is for you, my darling sweet
The one who's a gift like no other
The one who someday will know
What it is like to be mother.

Do not cry because of these words
But rejoice in God's promise
For what is taken away today
Will anchor tomorrow's solace

Date Night

You seat me at the table
An arranged setting with forks and knives
Never any plate, only a cup
I watch your hands as they ease my chair in place
The dark of the room hides your face
Sitting, you stare in my direction
The routine drains my cheeks and pales my complexion
You never speak so I can hear
Whispers make their way through and permeate the air
Experience then the tremendous flaw
Deliberate, I suppose for you, yourself to entertain
These whispers never reach me in time
No warning to get my house in order; my heart in line
No last opportunity to be valiant and kind;
Faithful nor just
Plus, never to say goodbye
How hopelessly brilliant you court us death...
How expensive your meals
You pay your bill with the cost of a life
No singular taste in cuisine revealed
So your dates keep guessing...
Where next, what next, how?
And why...
Only inadequate consolations given when they cry
When they leave the dining table broken by pain
Emptier as an individual than when they came
But you,
You only cash the cheque
And check you calendar.

Karina

I thought about you today
Remembered your commanding stare
'Come here little one,
Tell me your story'
And you would listen
With ears that drank in from the young and the grown
You knew no despise
Your ties were to your God
His people your co-workers
And what a work you did
With your words, we went on plane rides
Slides and sails atop the ocean floor
I remembered your silver hair in my grasp
Imperfect rows distracted by the truth in your words
Your last requests
Your forgotten regrets
Your love for God
I miss you Karina
But others can use a flight
Feel the breeze in their hair
And take the step to set sail
What a beautiful addition to His garden you are
How beautifully your petals glow
The pain never truly heals
But this much I know
You are home Karina
Home at rest

Today and Tomorrow

Today,
Hands extended for embrace
Cheeks wiped empty of tears
Many voices fill the place
Silence lost, and, for now,
Forgotten.

The box meets the earth
Darkness decorates the skies.
This is the only promise we had from birth
A rule we wished could be made an exception.

Tomorrow,
Those hands hold something else;
Cheeks are now damp with no wiping cloth
All the voices lost in space
Nothing but silence filling these empty rooms.

They have gone.
The mourners have left.
But I,
I am still here.

Short days

Short days by the river bank
    Feet teasing the leafy cold
    I see the glisten of sun rays bright
    Easy to forget the coming night

Short days picking lilies by the way
    Skipping without sandals or shoe
    Writing letters to leave by the window
    Of unspoken words old and new

Long days not envied to see
    The clouds darken to cry with me
    For if the days were treasure and gold
    No wish or duty will be left untold

Short days, be if you must
    For I have loved and toiled enough
    I will pack my pillow and blanket in a heap
    And dream of all the other days as I fall asleep

After

How curious a thing;
To experience joy after the sadness loss brings
How peculiar the feel of reverent bliss
Igniting a soul hosting the memories of the ones we miss

We brave the bleak weather of grief
Sheltered by a steady faith and supported belief
It is not that we forget the pain or the sorrow
But we have learnt to use hope to face the comfort that rides in
On the wings of tomorrow

Every day is different;
Some easier than others
Still, we greet them all
And slowly
Learn to make peace with death.

Battles Lost

She took the box from her mother.
Light from emptiness,
She carries the burden in her soul.
She kept it in the dark hollows of her mind;
A hidden place
Where no one could find it.
Then, a stranger stumbled into her heart
And found the weight of her mother's box
Pulling low.
He prodded and surveyed,
They reviewed and reinvented;
She lit candles for her peace
And took medicine for her heritage -
He built walls and ordered guards to keep her fears away,
Set up reinforcements to remind her she was safe –
But, even then it was too much, so she relented.
She got tired of the battle
And tired of the pain.
She took her mother's box
And buried it outside her window.
It was heavier now;
Inside were her children,
And though he wanted to be by her side;
To carry the shovel at least,
She left him by the mesh door,
Stepped out into the cold and dark
And there
She buried them alone.

In Spring

Maybe one day leaves won't fall from
Your eyes like they do
Maybe one day, there will be no more autumn
And this house won't be covered with the colors of your pain

Maybe one day we can skip winter
And shut the cold air out forever.

Maybe one day you will push through these doors
And gift a seed back to the earth;
We could watch it grow together.

Maybe one day you'll have strength enough to water it
I have a bucket I bought a while back.

When that happens,
If such a time ever does come,
Know that I will still be there in spring
Collecting green leaves instead of brown ones
And I will make a bed for us
At the roots.

Beyond the Wall

Can I go beyond the wall of my inner thoughts?
Crash against this icy fortress and find green on the other side?
Can I go beyond the wall of my tongue?
Climb through snow and blood and sweat and just stop talking
Just listen and laugh and be a smile ... Not just wear one?
Can I go beyond the wall of my anger?
Sleep after all my quests to escape and just rest
I'm too exhausted to fight and be upset and feel sad
I am weary because I miss her
I am weary because I hate the days I wasted when she was here
Can I go beyond the wall?
I'm tired of this side.
Too much ice.
Too much cold.

06.10

You looked so warm,
Smiling.
You fell asleep at peace;
I believe.
How stupid I must have been
So young and without any idea of what the future had in store
We were at odds
But I thought you would always be there
With me
Us
To see us grow
And watch us get better at taking on this world
But you did three times as much as any mother did in only one lifetime
Because of you
I believe in miracles and forgiveness
In devotion profound and fierce
In compassion that sacrifices regardless of opposing forces
Because of you, I saw strength in action
And love in the eyes of a woman who couldn't always use the lingo
But who embodied the truth of all that it is worth
How I loved you mommy
How we love you still
Forgive your daughter of her idiocy
Forgive me for the years I wasted.
And,
If you can,
Please wake up.

Untitled

She bled her despair through her wrists
Punctured veins polluted by loneliness and stolen virtue
She drained herself of pain
With every fading breath, she gave in to the numbness of it all
No more havoc to wreak
No more hurt to endure
She faded away with her inability to survive the destruction of her person
And her ability to destroy other persons
I wish I could have been there to stitch her wounds
To carry her on my shoulders into tomorrow
I wish she had reached out to someone
And that we were vigilant enough to see

She couldn't see beyond her today
I pray,
I beseech you please
Hold on beyond today
Hold on to find hope in tomorrow

Not For Me

They will say I lived a full life
[As preachers and visitors must offer this sentiment
To try and comfort a family met with grief]

And,
Perhaps I did

Still, there were moments when I was wildly unhappy
And insecure because I had not lived up to my potential
Yes,
I have taken some creativity to this wretched box with me
And I have intelligence and bravery that I can no more offer to this soil
Than I offered to the world in my time above ground

But, do not cry for me
    Put your sadness to better use

Cry for those who need your tears the most
And, after crying
    Help them live.

Time Ends

I was once afraid of you.
Now I sit, pen in hand,
Writing about your arrival.
I do not fear your kiss
I no longer quiver at the thought of your cheek resting on mine.
Why should I?
One day you will come for me
And no might, no quarrel, no will
Can force you away if my sands finally did stop falling.
I do hope you are gentle though;
That when you whisk me away
It is ballroom and lights-
Charming, and polite.
I hope I have the chance to whisper what I never had strength to utter
before
To the persons I most need to whisper to.
Give me that one last consolation
And I will buckle my shoes,
Meander my arm through the air
And poise my fingers in artistic display.
I will glide over to meet your grasp
Without apprehension
Or mortal cowardice,
And then,
When the chords are strung
And the lights go dim,
I will dance the night away with you
When time ends -
When my time ends.

A poem never ends -
Never says goodbye.
It leaves itself here,
To be picked up in a stanza
Tomorrow.

FIN

ABOUT THE AUTHOR

Jaevel is the youngest of three children born to Earl and Althia Morgan-Brown. She is an educator, youth service enthusiast and avid volunteer. Jaevel is a Christian and a member of the Linstead Baptist Church in her hometown in St. Catherine, Jamaica.

Printed in the United States
By Bookmasters